The Soldier

THE SPANISH-AMERICAN WAR SOLDIER AT SAN JUAN HILL

By Carl R. Green and William R. Sanford

Illustrations by George Martin

Edited by Jean Eggenschwiler
and Kate Nelson

PUBLISHED BY

Capstone Press

Mankato, MN, U.S.A.

Distributed By

CHILDRENS PRESS®

CHICAGO

CIP
LIBRARY OF CONGRESS CATALOGING IN PUBLICATION DATA

Sanford, William R. (William Reynolds). 1927-
The Spanish-American War soldier at San Juan Hill / by William
R. Sanford, Carl R. Green.
p. cm.-- (The Soldier)
Summary: Recreates the experiences of one soldier in the Spanish-
American War as he fights with Teddy Roosevelt and his Rough
Riders in the Battle of San Juan Hill.
ISBN 1-56065-003-6
1. San Juan Hill, Battle of, 1898-- Juvenile literature. 2. United
States. Army--History--War of 1898-- Juvenile literature. [1. San
Juan Hill, Battle of, 1898. 2. United States--History--War of 1898--
Campaigns.] I. Green, Carl R. II. Title. III. Series: Sanford,
William R. (William Reynolds), 1927- Soldier.
E717.1.S22 1989
973.8'9--dc20   **89-25136 CIP AC**

PHOTO CREDITS

The Roosevelt Collection, 21, 33

Illustrated by George Martin
Designed by Nathan Y. Jarvis & Associates, Inc.

Capstone Press

Box 669, Mankato, MN, U.S.A. 56001

CONTENTS

JOINING UP TO FIGHT FOR UNCLE SAM

After the American Civil War ended in 1865, most of the soldiers returned to civilian life. America did not want a large standing army. America felt safe behind its ocean barriers. The soldiers who stayed in uniform were sent to fight Indian wars in the west. By the 1890's the regular army numbered fewer than 30,000 officers and men.

Once in a while a politician would wonder, "How will we defend ourselves in the event of war?" For most Americans the answer was simple. The National Guard, the modern version of the Revolutionary War Minutemen, could be activated. These citizen soldiers trained on weekends and during the summer. If a major war developed, there was also another manpower pool waiting. Patriotic young men would volunteer to serve in the armed forces.

The need for volunteer soldiers came suddenly. As 1898 dawned, the U.S. and Spain were drifting toward war. The conflict grew out of Spain's mistreatment of the people of Cuba, Puerto Rico, and the Philippines. Americans read in their newspapers about Cuban rebels and pressured President William McKinley to help them. The war fever grew after the newspapers reported the horrors of Spanish rule in Cuba. The public's outrage climbed to a fever pitch after the U.S.S. Maine was blown up by a mine in Havana harbor. By late April the two nations were at war.

The United States Navy was ready when the war began. The army was not. Congress voted to build up the army by enlisting 125,000 volunteers. The call went out and young men from every state rushed to enlist.

Thomas Harriman was one of the first to volunteer. "Long Tom" was an 18-year-old cowboy from the Pecos Valley in New Mexico Territory. His nickname was a natural one.

Santiago de Cuba and the surrounding battle area.

Tom stood 6'3" and weighed a lean 160 pounds. When he took off his battered hat, he uncovered a mop of blond hair. His fair skin had been burned a reddish-brown by the sun. Born in Chicago, Tom had decided early that city life did not agree with him. When he was 15 he ran away from home and headed west.

Tom rode to Santa Fe with some other ranch hands to enlist. After he passed a brief physical exam, he was told to raise his right hand. An officer swore him into the army.

RECRUITING AN ARMY TO FIGHT IN CUBA

The new recruits shook hands and grinned proudly. They were not just everyday soldiers, not by a long shot. This was war, and they were members of the First Volunteer Cavalry. Nobody called the unit by its official name, though. The regiment was known throughout the country as the **Rough Riders**.

The men stayed in Santa Fe on their first night in the army. "I don't care how we got into this war," Tom told his new friends. "I was sick of eating chuckwagon grub and herding cows. If Uncle Sam wants to pay my way to Cuba, I'm ready."

The other men nodded agreement.

They were mostly young cowhands and ranchers. A few of the older men had been Indian fighters and buffalo hunters. "I'm all for helping the Cubans," Pete Jacobs said. "I just wonder if the Spanish really blew up the Maine. Are they that stupid? Once our battleship sank, the U.S. was certain to jump in with both feet."

"Heck, it could have been the Cuban rebels who sank the Maine," Whitey Simms put in. "Or maybe it was an accident. Who cares? Everybody blames the Spanish."

Tom listened intently. Down in the Pecos Valley, he hadn't heard much news of the coming war. He turned to one of the older men in the outfit. "Mike, what do you think?" he asked.

Mike scratched his chin and thought for a moment before he answered. "Some folks say this war is the work of that newspaper man, William Randolph Hearst," he said at last. "It started when Hearst was trying to outsell the other newspapers in New York City. He needed some exciting headlines so he sent reporters to cover the fighting in Cuba. Their stories about the cruelty of the Spanish really stirred up the public. Even then, there were lots of folks who did not want to get involved, including President McKinley. Why, it took Congress two months to declare war, even after the *Maine* went down."

A trumpeter blew "Taps" and the men crawled into their bedrolls. In all, 354 men had joined the Rough Riders in Santa Fe. Tom studied his companions and decided the Spanish did not have a chance. How could they stand up to these crack shots and expert horsemen?

A few days later the men were issued rifles and pistols. Tom's rifle was a **Krag-Jorgenson**, the regular cavalry carbine. He knew it was not the most modern weapon around, but it looked as though it would do the job. The Krag was a bolt-action .30-caliber rifle that had been invented in Denmark and improved in the U.S. It carried five bullets in its magazine and one in the chamber. Spanish troops, Tom heard, were equipped with modern German-made **Mauser** rifles. The Mausers fired high-velocity bullets and were very accurate.

As he practiced with the rifle, Tom found more to like about it. For one thing, the Krag weighed only eight pounds. Better yet, like the Mauser, it fired smokeless cartridges. The National Guard units were using single-shot Springfield rifles. Every time a soldier fired one, a puff of smoke from the black-powder cartridges gave away his position.

The Rough Riders trusted their officers as much as they trusted their guns. Colonel Leonard Wood commanded the regiment and

Lieutenant Colonel Theodore Roosevelt was second in command. The two men were working hard to give the regiment the best of everything. TR, as everyone called Roosevelt, did draw the line at issuing swords to the enlisted men. About all they would be used for, he said, was opening cans of beans. The Rough Riders wore blue shirts and brown canvas pants trimmed in cavalry yellow. A slouch hat, **leggings**, and boots completed the outfit.

In early May the volunteers from New Mexico left for San Antonio, Texas. Santa Fe gave them a noisy sendoff. By May 11 the unit was almost complete. Tom found himself in a unit beside Indians, polo players, college athletes, policemen, miners, and politicians. Colonel Wood organized them into three squadrons of four troops each. Each troop had three officers, eight sergeants, and at least 64 privates. The support troops included trumpeters, saddlers, blacksmiths, and wagoners.

Private "Long Tom" Harriman was assigned to Troop G. He was given a spirited bronco named Hotspur to ride.

TRAINING TO GO TO WAR

Tom liked Colonel Roosevelt right from the start. "Sure, TR grew up in the East, but he's lived out on the range," he told Pete one night. "Why, he can ride a bucking bronco as good as any of the boys."

Roosevelt had resigned as assistant secretary of the navy when the war started. The Rough Riders quickly learned that TR really cared about them. Typical was the day the colonel led two squadrons on a long, hard march. On the way back he ordered a halt near a beer garden. Smiling beneath his walrus mustache, he took the men inside and bought beer for everyone.

"This is going to be a bully war!" Pete

shouted. "Bully" was TR's favorite word. It meant everything was wonderful.

Colonel Wood was harder to get to know. He had been the White House surgeon before the war. Cool and cautious, he did not mix with the men like TR did. He worked hard to get them ready to fight.

Slowly the men's soldiering skills improved. They repeated the same drills hour after hour. "This isn't a game," a cold-eyed captain told them. "When you go into battle, doing things right may be the difference between life and death."

In the third week the orders everyone was waiting for came through. "We're moving out," Sergeant Butler told the troops. "Pack up what you can carry on your back and leave the rest."

Tom worked most of the night to load the horses and mules. At dawn the passenger cars pulled in. Tom's train was made up of ten coaches, a Pullman sleeping car for the officers, and a dozen horse cars. As usual, TR was everywhere, making sure that all went smoothly. When he found a private who was sick with the measles, he gave the man his berth in the Pullman. Later the coffee ran short, but TR made sure that more was found.

The trip east was tiring. Each time the train jolted to a stop, the horses had to be unloaded. Then the men fed and watered them and mucked out their stalls. Afterward, they reloaded the nervous animals and climbed back into the crowded coaches. No one got much sleep.

As the train headed into the South, Tom began to worry a little. "Look at this Yankee uniform," he told Pete. "Maybe it will make the Southerners want to fight the Civil War all over again."

Tom did not have to worry. At each stop the men were met with smiles and shouts of "Remember the Maine!" The high point of the trip for Tom came at a small town in Louisiana. There, a pretty Southern woman asked him for a souvenir uniform button. She paid for her prize by kissing him on the cheek.

After four long days, the regiment pulled into Tampa, Florida. Like the rest of the men, Tom had not shaved and he was wearing a dirty uniform. No one was there to meet them and no one knew where they were supposed to camp.

Colonel Wood took over. He marched the Rough Riders to a field two miles from the edge of town. Before long, tents were set up in neat rows, **latrines** were dug, and food was cooking. After a hot meal the men's spirits lifted.

Two days of drills on foot were followed by drills on horseback. Tom was happy to be back on Hotspur. The regiment paraded in front of General Nelson Miles, the army commander. Afterward Sergeant Butler told Tom that the officer with Miles was Joseph "Fighting Joe" Wheeler. The old Confederate general had been enlisted to ensure Southern support for the war.

Newspapermen and artists visited the camp to cover the war. Headlines soon reported that sickness was sweeping through the army. Sanitation was poor, and men were coming down with **dysentery**, typhoid, and the flu. Through it all, the railroad unloaded more men and supplies every day. A trainman said there were a thousand boxcars backed up on sidings farther north.

"Hey, Sarge, when are we going to Cuba?" Tom asked Sergeant Butler. "I'm dying in this hotbox."

"Moving an army isn't easy," Butler snapped. "There's only one rail line from here down to the port, and tourists use it during the day. The generals are working on the problem now."

Tom mopped his forehead. "After we lick the Spaniards," he joked, "maybe we can talk them into taking Florida back."

ON THE WAY TO CUBA

Everyone was shouting. "At ease!" Sergeant Butler roared. When the men fell silent he went on in a quieter voice. "There aren't enough ships to take all of the men and the horses. At least Troop G is going! A lot of Rough Riders would like to be in your boots."

The sergeant was right. Only eight troops were leaving with Wood and Roosevelt. The men in the remaining four troops complained bitterly about being left behind.

At 10 o'clock on the night of June 6, the Rough Riders moved out. Tom threw his white blanket roll over his shoulder. He carried his rifle, 125 rounds of ammunition, a canteen, mess gear, and a **haversack** for rations. The train that was supposed to pick them up at midnight never arrived. At six in the morning the impatient Rough Riders forced a coal train to stop. The soldiers climbed onto the coal cars and the train headed for Port Tampa.

More confusion awaited them at the port. General Shafter sent Wood and TR to Colonel Humphrey, the quartermaster in charge of embarking the troops. "Do you see those two ships about to dock?" Humphrey said, pointing to the channel. "Take one!"

TR sent the Rough Riders running to where the *Yucatan* was tying up. Two other units were already marching toward the ship, but the Rough Riders blocked the way. Moments later they had their gear stowed on board. Only then did they allow the soldiers from the 2nd Regiment to climb the gangway onto the ship.

Every bit of space on the Yucatan was filled. A seaman told Tom they were carrying twice the number of soldiers the captain had expected. In addition, the ship was loaded with horses, wagons, supplies, and two newsreel cameramen. TR wanted to be sure that the war was captured on film.

That night Tom stood in a long chow line with Pete. A weary cook handed them

Colonel Theodore Roosevelt

something called "canned fresh beef." Tom could eat just about anything, but he gagged on his first bite.

Pete looked at his plate. "This is good," he said, "except that it's stringy, tasteless, and smells like a chemical factory."

TR took one look and ordered the men to throw the "embalmed beef" overboard. Everyone cheered.

The Yucatan sat at the dock for two days. Then it moved out into the bay and dropped anchor again. Hot and bored, the men cooled off by swimming in the ocean. Navy cruisers arrived to escort the troop carriers. But still the fleet waited. Rumors of Spanish warships near Key West had to be checked out.

The invasion fleet finally sailed on June 14. By then the Yucatan carried a hand-lettered sign: STANDING ROOM ONLY. In spite of all the crowding and bad food, the men were in good spirits. A song spread from ship to ship. Thousands of men sang, "There'll be a hot time in the old town tonight."

On Friday, June 17, Tom saw the green coast of Cuba for the first time. By Sunday, when church services were held on deck, he was wondering if they would ever land.

22

Finally, on Monday, the *Yucatan* steamed toward shore. They were off the south coast at Daiquiri, 15 miles east of the port of Santiago.

On June 22 the navy bombarded the beach at Daiquiri with its big guns. When the dust cleared, there was no sign of Spanish resistance. The small boats promised for the landing did not show up, so the navy took over the job. Tom and his platoon rode to shore in a lifeboat towed by a navy launch.

After a wild ride through the surf the men reached the safety of the village's stone pier. The unit fell in and marched through Daiquiri. Some Cuban rebels were waiting to greet them. "They look like scarecrows," Tom whispered to Pete. "The newspaper stories had me thinking they were supermen."

"Where are the Spaniards?" Pete called to the rebels.

One of them spoke English. "They left when the shelling started," the man said. "Now they're at Siboney, seven miles down the coast." He split open a coconut and handed it to Tom. The sweet coconut milk tasted wonderful.

Three Rough Riders climbed a nearby hill. There, atop an empty Spanish army blockhouse, they raised the Stars and Stripes.

Camp was set up a few hundred yards inland. Tom and Pete rolled up in their blankets to sleep.

An hour later, the sound of a shot woke them. Tom clutched his rifle and felt his heart pounding in his chest. Then he heard men laughing.

"The sentry shot a land crab," Mike Smith yelled. "It's the first **casualty** of the war in Cuba!"

THE ADVANCE TO SIBONEY

A new rumor ran through the Rough Rider camp every hour or so. "The Spanish are advancing!" "We're moving out!" "The Spanish have given up!" "We're staying here for a few days!" The last rumor sounded good to Tom. He cut palm leaves and made himself a shelter. Then he stripped down and bathed in a swift-running stream. After two weeks aboard ship, it felt good to be clean again.

The men built campfires to cook their meals. The cooking smells drew the Cuban rebels. Tom shared his rations with the thin, ragged men. "It's a good thing we're here," he whispered to Pete. "These men are starving."

Early that afternoon Tom had to say good-bye to his shelter. General Wheeler ordered the Rough Riders to break camp.

They were told to advance to Siboney, which was already in American hands. Colonel Wood set a fast pace through the jungle.

Sweat soaked the men's shirts and ran into their eyes. They felt better when they saw that TR was walking, too. "I won't ride while my men are walking," Tom heard him say.

Tom was not much of a walker. His pack seemed to gain weight with every step he took. He stumbled and fell when it caught on a tree branch. Some of the men threw away their blankets and personal gear. A few dropped out, unable to keep up the pace.

It was dark when the weary men made camp near Siboney. They built cookfires only to see them sputter out in a heavy rain. Pete huddled under a tree. "With this much rain," he said, "Noah wouldn't have had to wait 40 days for his flood!"

Tom felt as though he had just dozed off when the wake-up call came. By six o'clock the Rough Riders were marching toward the crossroads of Las Guasimas. The men were certain they would soon see action. They tramped though knee-deep mud and slapped at flies, gnats, and beetles. Someone said that the trail was known as El Camino

26

Real, the Royal Road. "If this is the king's road, he must have a hog pen for a palace," Tom laughed.

The joking stopped when the column was three miles from Siboney. A soldier was lying next to the trail. As Tom passed, he saw the **machete** slash across the man's neck. He looked away quickly. Until this moment, the war had seemed like a big game. The dead man made it all too real.

Scouts reported that Spanish earthworks lay only 500 yards ahead. The column stopped while Colonel Wood talked over the situation. Suddenly, the air was filled with the whine of bullets from Spanish Mausers.

Tom dove into the high grass beside the trail. Bullets clipped branches and tore big gashes in the trees. Where were the Rough Rider's two machine guns? He felt better when orders came down the line from Captain Llewellyn. "Stay calm. Don't shoot till you see something worth shooting."

General Wheeler sent 130 regulars to attack the Spanish from the right **flank**. Tom moved forward with a squad of Rough Riders, firing as he ran. He never did see the men who were shooting at him. All at once the Spanish pulled back. The firing stopped.

General Wheeler dashed up, so excited he forgot which war he was fighting. "We've got the damned Yankees on the run!" he shouted.

The Rough Riders made camp and counted their casualties. Eight men were dead and 34 had been wounded. A work detail dug a long trench and buried the bodies. Later

that night the men gathered around campfires and talked about the battle in low voices. As they ate a meal of beans and canned tomatoes the men learned that Roosevelt was now commanding the regiment. Wood had been moved up to 2nd brigade to replace the ailing General Young.

On June 26, two days after the fight on the trail, the Rough Riders broke camp. They moved two miles closer to Santiago without meeting any resistance. TR told them to set up camp in a marshy, open spot near a stream. Other army units were camped nearby. In their off-duty hours Tom and Pete ate mangoes, bananas, and limes from the nearby groves.

From the camp, Tom could see smoke rising from enemy campfires. He pointed to the nearest hill, where some large kettles used for making sugar were visible. "According to Sergeant Butler, that's Kettle Hill," he told Pete. "Over there, to the south, is San Juan Hill. It's about 150 feet high. The Spaniards have a big blockhouse there. And there, beyond the hills, is Santiago."

"I see buzzards circling over Kettle Hill," Pete said.

"They're waiting for us to attack," Tom said with a grin.

THE ATTACK ON KETTLE HILL

"That General Shafter, he's a man and a half," Sergeant Butler observed. Tom and Pete laughed with him. At over 300 pounds, the general was almost too heavy to sit on a horse.

"He may be fat," Tom put in, "but he's a good man. He's aggressive and he knows how to make decisions."

Captain Llewellyn joined the group, and Sergeant Butler called them to attention. Llewellyn outlined General Shafter's battle plan. One force would open the battle by attacking the village of El Caney to the north. Victory there would open the way to the reservoir above Santiago. If the Americans cut off the city's water, it would have to surrender. The second attack would be directed at the

Spanish defenses on Kettle and San Juan hills. That was where the Rough Riders would fight.

On June 30 the regiment moved into line. TR positioned his men on El Pozo Hill in the ruins of a sugar mill. The attack on El Caney was set to begin at dawn.

The hammering of artillery awoke Tom at daybreak on July 1. He looked up to see dawn fading from a cloudless sky. "This is a great day for a battle!" he called to Pete. After splashing cold water on his face, he ate a breakfast of bacon, **hardtack**, and coffee. Behind the camp a battery of artillery opened up. The sharp smell of black powder stung his nose. The Spanish guns answered with a deadly shower of **shrapnel**. TR led the regiment forward to shelter in the underbrush at the base of the hill.

The artillery fire died out fifteen minutes later. The Rough Riders formed a column of fours and marched forward to the San Juan River. They splashed across a shallow ford and moved to the right. Spanish rifle fire peppered the trees around them.

Tom wondered if a Spanish marksman had him lined up in his sights. That's crazy thinking, he told himself. The unit was still moving toward Kettle Hill. Tom knew their orders were not very exact. "Drift right until you join up with Lawton's men from the El Caney attack," TR had been told.

Shrapnel again ripped through the leaves. Tom looked up to see a Signal Corps balloon floating overhead. It was towed by ropes and held by men on the ground. An officer in the balloon's basket was reporting Spanish positions. The Spanish turned their fire on the balloon. The exploding shells caught the Rough Riders in the open. Men screamed and fell all around Tom. A shell punctured the balloon and it sank slowly to the ground.

The Spanish rifle fire was increasing. Tom looked over at TR. Some of the Rough Riders had taken cover in the tall grass along the road. Others were still beside the river, crouched against the banks. TR rode his horse up and down the road, waiting for orders to advance.

The orders came through an hour later. The Rough Riders were told to assist the regulars in the assault on the two hills. TR selected Kettle Hill as his target. He mounted his horse and formed his men into a **skirmish line**. With a shout, the Rough Riders started forward. Two other regiments joined them.

Roosevelt and his Rough Riders.

As the Rough Riders surged toward the hill, they passed some men of the 9th Cavalry hidden in the grass. Their captain told TR that his orders were to stay there. The Rough Riders passed through their line and started up Kettle Hill. Tom kept his eyes on the blue polka-dot handkerchief tied to TR's hat.

Forty yards from the top of the hill the Rough Riders ran into a line of barbed wire. As TR dismounted, a bullet nicked his elbow.

Instead of stopping he climbed over the wire and waved for his men to follow. Tom and the other Rough Riders swept forward, howling like madmen. Above the sound of the rifle fire came the deep chatter of the American **Gatling guns**.

Tom heard later that a British observer who watched them could not believe his eyes. "They've got courage to spare," the officer said. "But those schoolboys are playing a deadly game!"

The Spanish fled as the Americans raced toward them. Tom shot one of them as he ran across the open space behind the hill. Then he turned to see that Troop G's flag was already planted on top of the hill.

"*Viva Cuba libre!*" someone shouted.

Tom joined in, feeling a little giddy. "Long live free Cuba!" he screamed.

ONE MORE HILL TO CLIMB

Tom stood on top of Kettle Hill, enjoying the moment of victory. An instant later a shell exploded overhead and sent him diving for cover behind one of the kettles. The Spanish gunners were using shells timed to explode in the air. Shrapnel pinged off the kettle just above Tom's head.

Below and to the left, Americans were storming up San Juan Hill. Tom heard TR telling the Rough Riders to fire at the Spanish soldiers atop San Juan Hill. He stretched out and looked for targets. All he could see were the dark heads of Spanish riflemen. His first shot went low. "Correct for distance!" he scolded himself aloud. On his fourth shot a Spaniard went down.

The heavy firing went on for ten

minutes. The noise of rifles, Gatling guns, and field artillery was deafening. Then came an order: "Cease fire! We don't want to hit our own men." Tom laid his rifle down and watched the dramatic scene unfold. The American infantrymen were climbing steadily upward. Their dark uniforms stood out clearly on the green hillside. A soldier carried an American flag that snapped smartly in the breeze.

TR yelled something and ran down the back side of Kettle Hill. "The colonel's going to help those fellows on San Juan Hill," Tom called to Pete. "We can't let him go by himself!"

Tom, Pete and three other Rough Riders followed the colonel. Almost at once Spanish sharpshooters picked off two of the men. TR realized the danger and turned back. More bullets whined past their ears as the men scrambled to safety.

When they reached the kettles, Tom waved his rifle. "We've got the Spaniards corralled," he cried. "Let's go brand them!"

TR now had orders to lead a charge up San Juan Hill. This time the entire unit followed him when he ran forward. The Spanish riflemen again made the Rough

Riders pay dearly for their advance. Tom saw Pete spin around and fall, holding his leg. A hospital corpsmen ran to him and worked desperately to stop the bleeding. Pete will be okay, Tom reassured himself. He has to be. Tom kept going.

The sound of firing from the Gatling guns brought a cheer from the charging men. The front rank was now within ten yards of the Spanish trenches. As Tom paused to reload his Krag, he saw two Spanish soldiers leap up to fire at TR. When they saw that they'd missed, they tried to run. TR blasted away with his revolver, killing one and missing the other.

The American units were scrambled now. Regular troops were fighting beside the Rough Riders. TR took charge and drove everyone past the second line of Spanish trenches. The Spanish were already pulling back from the top of the hill. Tom climbed the last few yards and looked down on the red tiled roofs of Santiago. The final Spanish defense line lay half a mile away.

As the men caught their breath and tended the wounded, a messenger arrived. The Rough Riders were ordered to hold on at all costs. A private climbed to the top of the blockhouse on San Juan Hill and pulled down the Spanish flag. The men who crowded around the flag drew fire from a Spanish **sniper**.

The battle turned into an artillery duel. Spanish shells screamed overhead and were answered by American guns. The defenders felt like sitting ducks on the grass-covered hilltop. TR ordered his troops to take cover just short of the crest. Tom looked around and counted only 50 Rough Riders. The rest of the force came from other units.

Some of the blue-uniformed soldiers began to drift to the rear. "We're going to rejoin our units," Tom heard one of them say. Before the man had taken a dozen steps, they ran into TR. Revolver in hand, the colonel promised to shoot anyone who retreated. "The colonel always keeps his word," the Rough Riders assured the men who slouched back to the line.

For a moment, it looked as though the enemy would counterattack. The advancing Spanish troops had little stomach for further fighting, however. A hail of accurate fire from the Rough Riders quickly drove them back. As night came on, the firing slowly died away. Everyone on the hill ate well that night.

Tom found large kettles of beef stew, rice, and peas in one of the blockhouses. TR patted Tom on the back of the head and said, "Long Tom, it's a grand time to be alive. A bully time!"

The Rough Riders dug in and waited. A counterattack never came. The Battle of San Juan Hill was over.

AFTER THE BATTLE

The capture of the two hills opened the way to Santiago. With the Americans closing in, the Spanish fleet sailed from the harbor two days later. The warships of Admiral Sampson's fleet were waiting for them. All of the Spanish ships were either sunk, damaged, or driven aground. On July 17 Santiago's 24,000-man garrison surrendered.

The Spanish-American War lasted only a few weeks longer. A week after Santiago surrendered, American forces occupied Puerto Rico. Out in the Pacific more territory was being added to the new American empire. The U.S. quickly annexed Hawaii, but the conquest of the Philippines took a little longer. Commodore Dewey had already defeated the Spanish fleet at Manila Bay.

Now American and Filipino troops joined forces to attack Manila. The city fell on August 13, and the Spanish surrendered the next day.

42

The United States and Spain had already signed a cease-fire on August 12. President McKinley's announcement of the armistice set off a wild celebration. The formal peace treaty was signed in Paris on December 10. The Spanish gave Cuba its independence and handed Puerto Rico and the Philippines to the United States.

Peace did not bring an end to the army's problems in Cuba. Yellow fever, malaria, and food poisoning were proving more deadly than Spanish bullets. Tom fell ill with malaria, but he shook off the fever after a few days. Many were not as lucky.

Faced with a growing public outcry, the army decided to bring the boys home. On August 8 TR led the Rough Riders aboard the steamer *Miami* at Santiago. A week later the ship docked at Montauk Point, New York. Tom grinned happily as he looked down at the cheering crowd that welcomed them. It felt good to be a hero.

The brief military career of the Rough Riders was coming to a close. The men set up camp where they were visited by President McKinley.

Tom was tired of army life. On September 13 he picked up his pay and left the service. His enlistment had lasted less than five months. Pete and Whitey invited him to visit New York and Washington with them, but Tom was homesick for New Mexico. With money in his pocket, he was planning to make a down payment on a ranch of his own.

GLOSSARY

Important Historic Figures

WILLIAM RANDOLPH HEARST (1863-1951)— American newspaper publisher. His reporting of the news from Cuba helped create the public's demand for war with Spain in 1898.

GENERAL NELSON MILES (1839-1925)—Commander-in-chief of the U.S. Army during the Spanish-American War.

LT. COLONEL THEODORE ROOSEVELT (1858-1919)—The inspirational leader of the Rough Riders during the Spanish-American War. TR, as he was called, later became the nation's 32nd President.

GENERAL WILLIAM SHAFTER (1835-1906)— Commanding general of the U.S. forces that invaded Cuba in 1898.

GENERAL JOSEPH WHEELER (1836-1906)—A former Confederate general who was recalled to duty in 1898. Wheeler commanded the brigade to which the Rough Riders were attached.

COLONEL LEONARD WOOD (1860-1927)—The original commander of the Rough Riders. He later served as military governor of Cuba from 1899-1902.

Important Terms

CASUALTY—Someone who is killed or wounded in a military action.

DYSENTERY—An infection of the lower intestines that causes pain, fever, and diarrhea.

FLANK ATTACK—A strategy by which an army tries to hit an opposing force on one of its unprotected sides.

GATLING GUN—An early form of the machine gun.

HARDTACK—Hard, unsalted crackers that were part of a soldier's rations during the Spanish-American War.

HAVERSACK—A canvas sack in which soldiers carried their rations.

KRAG-JORGENSON—The standard cavalry carbine issued to the Rough Riders in 1898. The Krag was a bolt-action .30-calibre rifle that fired six rounds before it needed reloading.

LATRINE—An army term for a toilet.

LEGGINGS—Laced canvas coverings that soldiers wore to protect their lower legs.

MACHETE—A large, broad-bladed knife designed for cutting sugar cane. The Cuban rebels used their machetes in close combat.

MAUSER—The powerful German-made rifle used by Spanish troops during the Spanish-American war.

ROUGH RIDERS—The popular name given to Teddy Roosevelt's First Volunteer Calvary during the Spanish-American War.

SHRAPNEL—An artillery shell filled with metal balls that is fused to explode above enemy troops.

SKIRMISH LINE—Troops who advance in a thin line to make the first contact with the enemy.

SNIPER—A sharpshooter who fires from a concealed position. Snipers try to pick off enemy soldiers one by one.